# The Relation

## By Sophia Brooke

# Table of Contents

*Funny business, a woman's career: the things you drop on the way up the ladder so you can move faster. You forget you'll need them again when you get back to being a woman.*

*It's one career all females have in common, whether we like it or not: being a woman.*

*Sooner or later, we've got to work at it, no matter how many other careers we've had or wanted.*

– Joseph L. Mankiewicz (1909-1993)
in *All About Eve*

# Chapter 1

## Do not casually suggest breakups

*"There are seldom regrets for what you have left unsaid." –*
Peggy Post

## Coffee with Sophia

*"I didn't mean it Sophia. All I wanted was for him to say that he didn't want a breakup either and that everything was going to be okay. He wasn't supposed to agree to the break up. What have I done Sophia?"* she sobbed.

She had carelessly suggested a breakup one more time and her boyfriend walked away for good.

She sipped her hot chocolate at a café on Madison Avenue as the first flurries of winter greeted New York City. It's going to be a pretty cold winter – right, that doesn't help.

## Thought of the day

*"I've had enough of this, I want a breakup."*

*"You know what, it's hard enough to deal with my stressful job, I really don't need this. Let's take a break."*

*"I'm not sure if this marriage is working out."*

Have you heard of Murphy's Law? It says that, 'Everything that can go wrong, will go wrong.' Life can be a bitch. It may just be one of those seasons in your life when you suffer from horrible bosses, awful colleagues, bickering parents, PMS, bad cab rides and the lack of sleep. You are completely broke and to top it off, you accidentally knock your Chinese take-out dinner off the table edge and spill *Coca-Cola* on your laptop just when you are about to watch Bridget Jones on Netflix.

Stresses on top of your usual dose of relationship issues can be overwhelming. Calling off the relationship to get some weight off your shoulder will seem the best way out, but very often, it isn't.

Suggesting breakups carelessly is like crying wolf. One day, it may happen. Each time you take a break from the relationship, your partner will feel increasingly insecure. He senses a growing threat of abandonment and begins to be less trusting. It is only wise that he stops investing emotionally into the relationship to protect himself from being hurt when you walk away.

There's this other thing – power. Whether we know it or not, we regularly test the power we have over our partner. In fact, some of you will admit to having used the threat of abandonment to gain an upper hand in the relationship. That can work in the short run, at the least. This psychological tactic gives you an illusion that you are in control and creates a constant struggle for power. Little do you realize that your partner is slowly but surely slipping away. Truth is, no one wins in a relationship when the other half loses.

Perhaps, what you really want to say is simply this – *"I've had enough **for now**, let's talk tomorrow."*

**Lessons Learnt**

The easiest thing to do when you are stressed, angry or hurt is to suggest a breakup and walk away. It may seem a great idea in the heat of the moment but carelessly suggesting a breakup erodes trust and harbors insecurities. Especially when you feel particularly upset and are overpowered by a strong urge to break things off, don't. Hold that thought for three days and decide if that's still what you want afterwards.

## Chapter 2

## If you can't think of anything good to do, do nothing

*"The only DIY haircut I would ever recommend is a crop with the clippers: mess around with scissors and you'll regret it.' – Charles Worthington*

**Coffee with Sophia**

I walked briskly through Central Park towards a friend's apartment at West End. She had a fight with her fiancé and had apparently called off the engagement.

*"I prepared a nice birthday dinner for Luke last night with his favorite wine and all. I started to talk about the dinner menu for our wedding and he joked that he could use being a bachelor for another year or two. We ended up in a really huge fight and I tore our engagement invitations, broke the crystal dining set that his mother gave us and cut the diamond ring into three pieces."*

*"How did you cut the ring into three pieces?!" I asked.*

*"With the pliers in the storeroom. I wish I hadn't done that Sophia, what got into me?"*

**Thought of the day**

Anger, rage, hurt – you know those.

You stop thinking, you react and you hit back hard. You are over-powered by stress hormones – adrenaline, cortisol, norepinephrine – that trigger the fight or flight responses. You've been emotionally hijacked and the logical part of your brain stops being in control. A reactive attack will seem the most appropriate response when you aren't thinking clearly. But trust me, it isn't.

A gentleman shared that he once fought with his wife and she got so angry that she lost it and broke the sink in their bathroom to pieces with a sledgehammer. He had never seen that side of her before and was very shocked. Lucky enough for them, they have since moved past it but he admitted that it won't be easy for him to look at her the same way he did before that evening.

*'The hand is the visible expression of the mind.'* We are not responsible for our hearts but we are responsible for our actions. What you think matters less than what you do. When threatened, besides the fight or flight responses, there is always one more option – freeze.

**Lessons Learnt**

When you are filled with rage, you are your biggest enemy. The impulse to do something destructive can be compelling. But you know what? Don't.

Victory over self, is the toughest kind of victory. Rather than focusing your energy to manage situations and other people, try managing yourself. Staying still can be the hardest thing to do, especially when you are upset. So, when you find yourself in that state - do nothing. Yes, you heard me – freeze, at least for now.

## Chapter 3

### Love is a verb

*"Love is not what you say, but what you do." – John Hagee*

### Coffee with Sophia

I love weekend brunches with a few good friends in
Manhattan, or anywhere else in the world really. We picked
a corner table in a cozy restaurant at Upper West Village
and my attention shifted towards a mature couple seated
right across us. The elderly man was on a wheelchair and
his wife would help him occasionally with his food and
coffee. His hands tremored mildly and he spilt some coffee
on himself. She looked at him lovingly and gently wiped off
the brown liquid dripping from his chin onto the white table
cloth with her napkin.

One of our friend, a busy senior executive in a large
corporation excused himself shortly to call his fiancée in
Hong Kong. When he returned to the table, he apologized
and explained, *"We've been dating for over four years and
three of it were long distance. I call her every day before
she sleeps."*

*"Don't you sometimes have to miss the calls given your full
schedule?"* I asked.

*"Not really. That's something that we have agreed to stick
to. I'm also doing that for her, it makes her happy and she*

*feels better. If that makes her happy – calling her for twenty minutes or an hour a day - it's simple enough. I won't lie and say that I don't sometimes have to go out of my way to make these calls happen. When I travel across time zones, it can get tricky. But a man has got to do what he's got to do. If I can't even do that for her, she should probably not agree to marry me."*

Impressive.

**Thought of the day**

Saying *'I love you'* is easy, though, love is not just a feeling but a verb.

Love is what you do for your partner, the choices and decisions that you make every day that will affect your partner, even when he is not around you. Making that conscious decision to listen, sacrifice, forgive, empathize, reassure and appreciate. Deciding to have faith in your partner, avoiding the temptation of being alone with another man, controlling yourself, improving your communication skills to better your relationship, cheering him up when he is down, making the effort to understand him, or building relationships with the people he cares about; the list goes on.

What are some of the things that you do to show him that you love him?

1.  Do you manage yourself and avoid giving him a tough time frequently?

2. Do you forgive him quickly or do you choose to punish him just to prove a point?
3. Do you go the extra mile to take care of yourself so that you can better care for your partner?
4. Do you take the time to learn how you can communicate better with your partner?
5. Do you put yourself in his shoes when you can't see eye to eye?
6. Do you try to understand how men and women are different and how your relationship can benefit from this knowledge?
7. Do you willingly give to your partner or are you often selfish?
8. Do you frequently put your needs above your partner's?
9. Does your partner's emotion matter less than yours?
10. Do you make it a goal to make him happy or is your happiness more important than his?
11. Do you make extra effort to learn about your partner's likes and dislikes?
12. Do you exercise care in respecting your partner's boundaries?
13. Do you take time to understand why your partner may sometimes be insecure, upset or angry?
14. Do you try to calm down when you have disagreements or do you escalate these into shouting matches?
15. When emotionally charged, do you make a conscious effort to ask for a proper time out, or do

you simply walk out on him and block his access to you?

16. Have you taken time to learn about fighting fair?
17. Do you contribute to your relationship and your future together?
18. What are the top five challenges that you face in your relationship currently? What have you done to help solve these challenges? How are you supporting your partner play a role in resolving these issues?
19. What are your top three weaknesses that may lead to potential short- and long-term problems? These can range from spending too much time at work, self-imposed isolation, sustaining health deteriorating habits, gambling etc. What do you do about these to protect your relationship from yourself?
20. Have you been willing to manage yourself so that you can be a better partner?
21. What do you think of your love for your partner so far – is it a noun, or a verb?

**Lessons Learnt**

Love is not just a feeling but a verb. Your active participation, efforts, choices and actions tells your partner how much you love him. Saying *'I love you'* without behaviors and actions to back it up is often not enough. If you can't bring yourself to act, then you probably don't love him enough to want to do so.

# Chapter 4

## Be quick to forgive

*"The things two people do to each other they remember. If they stay together, it's not because they forget; it's because they forgive." – Demi Moore in Indecent Proposal*

**Coffee with Sophia**

"Good morning my love."

Your partner greeted you gently with a soft kiss on your forehead. He made your favorite breakfast and left it at the bedside table. You almost softened to his kiss when you recalled that you fought the night before. You were tempted to ignore him and punish him for not having managed to book the movie tickets as promised.

He sensed your apprehension and persuaded gently, *"I'm sorry love. Why don't we just let it go and enjoy our Sunday? We have both had a busy week, we can at least try and enjoy the remaining half of our weekend together?"*

**Thought of the day**

It is not uncommon for people to sometimes treat their partners worse than they would friends, colleagues and family. Many have squandered precious days in a relationship by refusing to forgive and choosing to punish their partners instead. You punish your partner when you give him the silent treatment, refusing to pick up calls, and rejecting him when he reaches out to make peace. You are angry, upset and hurt, and you want him to feel what you feel.

Not forgiving, at best, and being vindictive, at worst, can ruin your relationship.

1.  Do you often carry fights over to the next day?
2.  How long do you hold on to grudges before you forgive him?
3.  Do you often bring up ALL his faults in arguments?
4.  Has he always been the one to first apologize?
5.  Do you find yourself 'punishing' him frequently?
6.  Do you feel that your inability to forgive your partner is scarring your relationship?
7.  Do you feel that your inability to forgive your partner is creating distance in your relationship?
8.  Does your partner tell you that he feels like he is walking on egg shells in your relationship?
9.  Do you nitpick often?
10. Do you harp on about his mistakes repeatedly?

It is important to forgive your partner quickly as all sorts of disagreements and frictions will happen over the course of your relationship. Choosing to forgive quickly doesn't mean that you are getting the short end of the bargain. The alternative is to not forgive, but that is equal to punishing him. He will feel hurt even if he doesn't show it.

Everyone will make mistakes but the true test to a man's character is how he recovers from it. If you truly love him, forgive him.

**Lessons Learnt**

Be quick to forgive, there's something to be said for second chances.

# Chapter 5

## Minimize fighting, pick your battles, fight fair
*"A cobra spits only when it has to." – Sophia Brooke*

### Coffee with Sophia

I waited for my next flight at the JFK International Airport in New York. I had just gotten in from the freezing cold in Boston and was looking forward to the sunny weather in Asia. *'Twenty more hours to Singapore, shouldn't be too bad,'* I cheered myself on. While waiting to get on my next flight, I decided to read a crumpled printout given to me last month by a friend who has a psychology practice - "The Fight Fair Contract". Interesting.

In an interview with a lady in her sixties earlier that week, she told me that though she loved her partner very passionately, she had also fought him quite fervently. She admitted that many of the fights were unnecessary and were over issues that mattered little to both. These fights had led them to exchange unkind words, hurt her partner, and scarred their relationship.

*"Minimize fighting,"* she said. *"Sticks and stones may break your bones but words, I tell you, words can hurt like hell and you cannot take them back. Pick your battles. If you must fight, fight fairly."*

**Thought of the day**

Most couples will have at least a few intense fights sometime no matter how much they love each other. A healthy dose of fights can be helpful for couples to get know one another better and can at times, bring the pair closer. However, if they develop a pattern of getting into regular and protracted fights, these clashes can spiral out of control.

Like it or not, frequent arguments in your relationship can eat away the affection your partner has for you. Think about this, after a long day of work and having to deal with demanding bosses and colleagues, will a man look forward to going home to a discontented, unhappy and bickering partner? No longer a source of happiness, stability and emotional support, a relationship filled with constant discord can become totally draining.

1. Have you been fighting frequently with your partner?
2. How often do you try to defuse your fights before they escalate?
3. What do you usually argue about?
4. Can these issues be resolved peacefully?
5. Do you fight fairly?
6. A hard start to a fight often leads to a hard landing; and a soft start tend to result in a somewhat cushioned landing. Do you consciously begin your

conflicts softly and try to steer it back to a soft confrontation when you sense an escalation?

7. Do you often raise your voice or speak harshly at your partner when you have a disagreement?

Frequent and unhealthy fights, left unchecked, often lead to relationships breaking down. It is important that you fight fairly and keep your side of the bargain.

Rules outlined in the Fight Fair Contract:

1. I will arrange an appropriate time with my partner to have a discussion when both are feeling fresh and relaxed. I will not start a difficult discussion when either of us are too hungry, angry, lonely or tired.
2. I will think before I speak or act. Before starting to discuss a difficulty in the relationship, I will ask myself, "How important is it". We all know that the vast majority of such difficulties are over something that is trivial.
3. I will use a softened start up and not a critical attack on my mate.
4. I will make no dramatic exits.
5. I will be respectful of my partner.
6. I will listen carefully.
7. I will use "I" statements and not "you" statements to avoid blaming and generalizing.
8. I will keep my statements short.
9. I will stick to the current issue or problem, I will not bring up baggage from the past.

10. I will constantly remember that my objective is to come to a mutually acceptable solution.
11. When confronted unexpectedly, or if my emotional reaction becomes too strong, I will use emotional regulation strategies such as
    a. Stop, Breathe Deeply, Reflect
    b. Positive self-talk e.g. "I can handle this"
    c. Time-out procedure

**Lessons Learnt**

Frequent fights can undermine your relationship. Minimize fighting and pick your battles wisely. If you must fight, then, fight fairly.

## Chapter 6

## Don't indulge in the blame game
*"If you behave in a manner that poisons your relationship, don't be surprised when it dies." – Steve Maraboli*

### Coffee with Sophia

It was a lovely afternoon in Singapore. I treated myself to a big delectable piece of banana chocolate chip cake drizzled with butterscotch sauce at the P.S. Café overlooking the lush green rainforest plants in Dempsey. I did not mean to eavesdrop on the conversation of a couple seated at the next table as their quarrel escalated.

*"It's your fault. You never consider how I feel and always think only of yourself. You are so selfish!"*

Whatever the argument was about, both seemed to use these words repeatedly – you, always, never, your fault.

### Thought of the day

In another fight, a girl had discovered a few message threads with several ladies in her boyfriend's mobile. She got into a fit and accused him of cheating. The guy turned the table and reproached her instead for meddling with his phone and for intruding into his privacy!

Okay, let's admit it. We have all been guilty of blaming our partner for all sorts of things even when it wasn't really his fault. Sometimes, we do not even realize that we are doing that.  I'm not saying that you should evade discussions altogether though.

Just be very careful not to fall into the trap of blaming your partner for what you are responsible for. There are a lot of things that you are accountable for – your own happiness, needs and mistakes. Do also be mindful to not blame him for stresses that other people – in-laws, friends, your boss, strangers - have caused, especially those that he has no control of whatsoever.

**Lessons Learnt**

Don't indulge in the blame game. Use less of these words – you, always, never, you should, your fault – and think of how you can do things differently to resolve a predicament than to be too quick blame to your partner.

# Chapter 7

## Do not cheat

*"Cheating and lying aren't struggles, they're reasons to break up." – Patti Callahan Henry*

### Coffee with Sophia

*"I walked into our room and saw the two of them in bed. It's not something that I can forget, nor forgive. How can he do that to me, to the children? I felt my head spinning and my world collapsing around me."*

I didn't know what to say.

### Thought of the day

Men tend to get away with bad behaviors when they have options, so do women. But cheating is more than just a reckless behavior. Cheating is a betrayal of trust, a deliberate act of deceit. In fact, infidelity is one of the top most-cited reason for divorces and breakups.

*"Trust is the foundation that a relationship is built on and integrity is what you do when no one is watching. A relationship is nothing if there is an absence of trust. Once it is broken, the relationship will not be the same again."*

There are very few things worse than for a man to learn that the woman he loves is in bed with another. But why do women cheat? Among other things, loneliness, temptation, need for confidence boost, lack of sexual intimacy and lack of excitement. No matter what that is, it is just not good enough a reason to cheat.

Many of you also have jobs that require you to mingle with internal corporate stakeholders and spend time with clients. An innocent drink with a man alone in the evening or a harmless flirt may turn into something else if a woman lets her guard down. Networking in a male-dominated world puts women in vulnerable positions as they try to find their footing professionally. Powerful bosses, clients and investors demanding sexual favors from women in subordinated positions is not unheard of.

These men prey on women with partners or women with their careers at stake as they know that discretion is practically guaranteed. As societies and leaders continue to let promiscuous males at workplaces get away time and again, they are less kind to women. You will have everything including your reputation to lose.

Cheating hurts, and can cost you your relationship, don't cheat.

**Lessons Learnt**

Avoid temptation, remain faithful and don't cheat.

# Chapter 8

## The tale of two planets – not drifting apart
*"A successful marriage requires falling in love many times, with the same person." – Mignon McLaughlin*

### Coffee with Sophia

An intelligent and successful ex-Wall Street banker once shared with me about an almost perfect marriage he had that ended up in a divorce.

*"I had everything I wanted – a beautiful wife, an amazing child, lots of money and a very successful career. We were the perfect couple in college. I made my money early in life and achieved my career goals way ahead of my peers. People envied us."*

*"But somewhere along the way, we both got too busy with work and the kids, we just drifted apart."*

### Thought of the day

A wise CEO of a Silicon Valley tech company once told me about the tale of two planets. He interlocked the thumb and index finger on his left hand to that on his right hand to form two interlocking rings.

*"Have you heard of the tale of two planets? These two planets have an orbit each. The point at which the orbit*

*overlaps indicate their shared path. Every day, the man will travel around his own orbit. This orbit represents his daily journey in life, work and experiences separate from that of his partner. Every night, he will return home to his partner and spend quality time communicating to her about his trials, triumphs and growth. This way, although they go about their daily lives as unique individuals, they touch base at night so that they do not drift apart."*

Each of our orbits will vary in size and texture. This alludes to the different degree of challenges faced and efforts needed to complete your day. Like the planets, some of you may spin around your orbits faster than your partner. You may have grown up in a different culture or country, and will likely view the world with lenses that are dissimilar to that of your partner's. You need to consider that your partner and you will have different career prospects, personal development opportunities and growth rates. These differences, if not shared, can sometimes lead couples to drift apart. It is important to communicate daily, listen, empathize, reaffirm and make time for each other.

Now, the big picture. The twin planets share a main orbit, like that of earth's, which takes it around the sun. This orbit represents the pair's shared "Life Direction". Regularly communicating your experiences with your partner can in part, help you stay on the same page and save you from drifting apart.

**Lessons Learnt**

Make time to listen, communicate and connect with your partner every day. If your intuition tells you that you are drifting apart, don't wait too long to get your relationship back on track.

## Chapter 9

**If you have nothing good to say, say nothing**
*"Speak when you are angry and you will make the best speech you will ever regret." – Ambrose Bierce, The Devil's Dictionary*

### Coffee with Sophia

*"I ordered a glass of wheat beer at the beer garden. Not so long ago, someone I loved dearly was seated right across me at that same table. I could not help thinking about all the things that I had said to him when I was frustrated, disappointed and hurt. I did not mean them and have regretted saying them, he was deeply hurt. We have since parted ways and though I know that I shouldn't have too many regrets in life, I still wonder if things would have turned out differently if I was able to hold my tongue that day."*

### Thought of the day

Have you ever said hurtful things you wish you never did to your partner?

It can sometimes seem a good idea to speak your mind, your discontent and how you feel. This is especially true when you feel fearless after a glass of beer or two, it's now or never. Bad idea. Be that communication verbal, via

WhatsApp, or Facebook (very bad idea, for real) – there can be serious consequences to your relationship.

Contrary to what you think when you are not sober or angry, you can't take back what you have said. Your messages can be as short as *'Please don't contact me again, ever'*, *'I hate you'*, *'Leave me alone'* or *'I regret the day we got together'*. These words cut deeper than knives and can push him away.

When you have nothing good to say in that moment, it's probably best to not say anything. Especially when you are drunk, angry, upset, tired, hungry, unwell or frustrated – you tend to care less about the consequences of what you say then, but you probably will change your mind afterwards. Let the dust settle and take some time to gather your thoughts before making that speech.

**Lessons Learnt**

Silence can really be golden at times. What you say to others is often irrevocable. Say what you mean. If you don't mean it, don't say it.

# Chapter 10

## Communicate, communicate, communicate – but, do learn to communicate well

*"The single biggest problem with communication is the illusion that it has taken place." – George Bernard Shaw*

### Coffee with Sophia

From one of my favorite movies – *'P.S. I love you'*:

Woman: *"I know what you're really saying even when you don't say it"*
Man: *"You mean the two conversations thing. The one we're having and the one you think we're having."*

Communication is not only about what you say, but also, what you don't say; it's not only about what you do but also, what you don't do. Communication is more than the content you say. How you say it, the tone you use, the words you choose, your body language, the look in your eyes; all these matters.

### Thought of the day

Communication breakdown is one of the commonest reasons for divorces and breakups. When we communicate with our partner, a few things take place:

1.  You think of what you want to say

2. You say it and think that it is what you said
3. What you actually said
4. What your partner heard
5. What you think your partner heard
6. What your partner actually understands about what he's just heard

Indeed, that one sentence can go wrong in so many ways.

Now, let's look at the things that can lead to a communication breakdown in a relationship.

1. Saying what you don't mean
2. Not communicating openly in fear of offending your partner
3. Stop communicating due to busy schedules
4. Not making time to communicate
5. Reluctance of either or both to honestly speak to their preferences
6. You may often take things personally or may be too sensitive to constructive feedback. This can lead to problems accumulating over time and your partner will start to feel like he is walking on eggshells
7. Lack of a 'safe environment' to communicate honestly
8. You have established a pattern of using negative vocabulary
9. You have established an unhealthy pattern of communication and are not making a conscious effort to break the loop

10. Either or both lack the understanding that communication requires conscious effort
11. Expecting your partner to know you well enough to read your mind
12. Not taking the time to listen to your partner
13. Frequently blaming your partner for issues in your relationship
14. You do not honor your promises
15. You avoid difficult conversations
16. You delay difficult conversations that leads to your partner experience emotional suffering more than the issue deserved due to your inability or willingness to engage
17. You stonewall – stonewalling is the termination of communication as you block access of your partner to you altogether
18. Lack daily communication to maintain an open and healthy line of communication. This later leads to couples drifting apart

Learning to communicate in a relationship is like teaching a toddler. You will need to create a safe environment and help your new relationship develop a common language that you can both understand. Below, some ideas.

1. Learn how to communicate well in a relationship
2. Practice communication with your partner
3. Maintain a healthy set of vocabulary
4. Avoid blaming your partner – reduce the use of 'you', 'always', 'never', 'you should', 'your fault'

5. Do not judge
6. Avoid being defensive
7. Encourage open communication
8. Do not avoid conflicts – make provisions for 'healthy fights'
9. Do not stone wall, keeping silent can cause resentment to build over time
10. Take time to resolve conflicts instead of letting the conflicts accumulate over time
11. Avoid having double standards
12. Create a safe environment for honest communication – do not attack your partner when he shares his views, feedback, preferences and concerns
13. Restore open and healthy modes of communication as soon as you realize that you have derailed. Make a conscious decision to break unhealthy communication patterns
14. Do not let bad communication habits persist in your relationship – passive aggressive behaviors, regular outbursts, stone-walling, shouting matches, avoiding conflicts, silent treatment, contempt, patronizing and condescending behaviors, disrespect, denigrating and demeaning your partner
15. Focus on your aligning your common interest and solving the issue at hand and do not dig up the past or attack your partner's personality or under the belt.
16. Let him know that you love him, every day

Cultivating healthy channels of communication in your relationship is like building a house. It is easier to build it right the first time.

**Lessons Learnt**

Communication is one of the basic building blocks in a relationship. Make time to communicate and when you do, put in some effort to do it well.

## Chapter 11

### Keep skeletons where they should be, in the closet
*"Let not your past haunt or define you, but let it be a part of who you can become."*

**Coffee with Sophia**

"*She hacked into my phone, read messages and emails from my exes from ages ago. We have already had a ridiculous fight about my past. And each time we fight, she will dig up my past, raise these ghosts from their graves and give them flesh to walk all over our relationship. It is absurd.*"

**Thought of the day**

Some of you can move on from your past easily while others make the mistake of taking out your skeletons from your closet a little too often, too early and in too much detail.

Worse still, comparing your partner with your exes – finances, physical attributes, personalities, performance in bed. Just as much as you dislike being compared to an ex-girlfriend, avoid comparing your partner to your ex. It can be very unpleasant and can lead to insecurities and distance in your relationship.

As you go from one relationship from the other, you may collect lessons learnt and it can become almost intuitive to compare your current partner to your exes. Though it may be good to share about your past relationships with your current partner honestly, it can sometimes serve you well to just dig a hole and bury your past.

Don't rehash his past. Don't indulge in reminiscing the wonderful moments you have spent with your ex. He is your ex for a reason and he should stay as that. There is no point fighting over his past or yours as both your exes would have long moved on with their lives. It is time for you to move on from yours as well.

**Lessons Learnt**

Sometimes, to let go, we must leave something behind so that we can move forward.

# Chapter 12

## Understand his language of love

*"Saying I love you in a language of love your spouse does not understand, is like, handling the works of Shakespeare to an ape." – C.S. Huey*

**Coffee with Sophia**

My friend ordered several local dishes at the *Tsui Wah 'Cha Chaan Teng'* (local tea restaurant) in Hong Kong as we caught up with each other. Thankfully, she had much to say as the tasty but spicy noodles paralyzed my tongue and probably seared the insides of my mouth.

*"I have dated several successful men. They often bought me gifts and took me to expensive restaurants. But I wanted them to spend time with me and to make time to communicate with me. I usually stick to my few favorite handbags and shoes anyway, one more bag won't make me much happier."*

*"So, I moved on to dating men with stable jobs minus the jet-setting lifestyle. And you know what? Some had no ability or willingness, to understand my language of love. At the end of the day, I think it boils down to the person. Even if he claims to love you but can't bring himself to learn about the different languages of love, what yours are and share his openly, it's going to be an uphill battle. To some*

*extent, it reflects his attitude and values – will he go out of his way to make things work in your relationship? Is it all about him? Will he be a collaborative team player in your relationship or will you always have to be the one who gives in to him? Is he a giver, or a receiver? Is he willing to grow and become a better person, a better partner?"*

**Thought of the day**

We each express and perceive love differently. It is important that you are aware that your partner may have a love language that is different to yours. In his book, "The Five Languages of Love", Gary Chapman categorized these languages into five groups:

1. Words of affirmation
2. Quality time
3. Receiving gifts
4. Acts of service
5. Physical touch

Find out what his language of love is and whether he has a second language of love. Help him understand yours. If your partner's primary language of love is *'physical touch'*, it doesn't matter you tire yourself out doing things for him or if you flood him with gifts, he will not feel as loved as when you shower him with affection, hugs, kisses and cuddles.

**Lessons Learnt**

Take the time to find out what your partner's language of love is and let him know what yours is. This way, you will be able to love each other in a way you can both appreciate.

# Chapter 13

## Maintain a healthy vocabulary in your relationship
*"A bad word whispered will echo a hundred miles." –*
*Chinese Proverb*

### Coffee with Sophia

Man: *"Can you stop being a psycho and shut your motherfucking mouth up?"*
Woman: *"Stop calling me a psycho, you're such a jerk! Leave me alone and get the fuck out of my house."*
Man: *"Bitch. Fuck you."*
Woman: *"Ain't getting any asshole, fuck off!"*

### Thought of the day

Many of us have an arsenal of unhealthy vocabulary that we have collected over the years. We must be conscious not to use it recklessly. The minute a couple starts to use profanity against each other, they set a precedent and allows for an unhealthy pattern of using unsavory words to form.

It is important that we are cognizant of our use of language and not make character assassinating, invalidating or abandoning threats at our partner. Do you use any of these phrases carelessly at your partner?

1. Jerk, asshole, son of a bitch
2. I hate you, damn you

3. Liar, psycho, crazy
4. Fuck you, fuck off etc.
5. Coward, pussy
6. Stupid, moron, idiot, dim wit, twat, retarded
7. Go away, leave me alone
8. You get the idea…

Hostile venting is very damaging to your relationship and can be very hurtful. The longer you allow for the use of negative vocabulary to carry on in your relationship, the more destructive it becomes. Self-awareness and restraint when it comes to the choices of words in our relationships are paramount, particularly in cases when you are emotionally charged.

If you catch yourself doing it, work with your partner and make a conscious decision as a team to break the pattern.

**Lessons Learnt**

Maintain a healthy set of vocabulary and actively remove negative phrases in your relationship. A habit of using unhealthy vocabulary can develop over time, resulting in mutual character assassination, disrespect and the breakdown in communication.

# Chapter 15

## Protect your relationship
*"He who fears danger will not perish by them." – Leonardo Da Vinci, Thoughts on Art and Life*

### Coffee with Sophia

Relaxed, with my back against the comfortable chair at the *Peshwa Pavillion* lobby restaurant, I took time to admire the grand composition of the luxurious interiors of the ITC Maratha Hotel. In Mumbai, the air-conditioning can be a godsend. I sat across my guest as she shared her story with me.

*"I don't remember the number of times when I have been careless about exposing my relationship to all sorts of assaults. We had countless fights. We argued about our families, the types of washing liquid to use, taking out the garbage, doing the dishes, making the bed, our finances, our friends. We also sabotaged ourselves with fights due to jealousy, selfishness and ignorance."*

*"At times, I would consult my friends and family. I had unknowingly placed our fate in their hands. How silly is that. They had no context and they knew nothing about my husband. I neglected my responsibility to protect his feelings and repeatedly sabotage our relationship. Honestly*

*Sophia, the biggest threat to my relationship has often been myself."*

**Thought of the day**

Imagine a sacred ground that is surrounded by a protective circle that ringfences it from the outside world. That patch of sacred ground, represents your relationship. In order to maintain peace and stability, you need to be wary of things that you let come between your partner and you. This includes your friends, parents, in-laws and other family members. Do not be surprised if the threat is sometimes, yourself.

What are some of these common threats?

1. Temptation to cheat
2. Careless use of hurtful words
3. Unchecked mood swings
4. Dysfunctional personal finance management
5. Addiction – alcohol, drugs, gambling, compulsive spending behaviors
6. Unaddressed insecurities and low self-esteem
7. Punching him below his belt
8. Emasculating words and actions
9. Excess pessimism and negativity
10. Verbal or physical abuse
11. Stone-walling, passive aggressive behaviors
12. Unhealthy communication styles
13. Constantly allowing interference by parents, siblings, family members, friends or even children

14. Distrust, disrespect, being unkind or vindictive
15. Work stresses

If you have reasons to believe that you are sometimes a menace in your relationship, it will be helpful to discuss this openly with your partner. Figure something out as a team or seek help from relationship counselors.

## Lessons Learnt

We are often unaware of the harm that is directed at our relationship by others or by ourselves. People who love us, albeit having our best interest at heart may lack the context to give you the right prescription. Protect your relationship.

# Chapter 16

## Violence, abuse – a no go
*"Violence is not acceptable in a relationship, period."*
*Sophia Brooke*

**Coffee with Sophia**

*"Wait a minute, did you say that he blocked you from getting out of the house? And that he grabbed you to restrain you, shook you and shoved you after?"*
*"Yeah, why?"*
*"Did you know that that's physical abuse? Are you really going to marry him?"*
*"Oh, I thought it's only physical abuse if he hits me…"*
*"Seriously…?!"*

**Thought of the day**

Violence of any kind is not acceptable in a relationship.

Some women make excuses for their abusers and live in denial. Violence is inexcusable. If your partner has threatened to hurt you, intimidate you or exert physical violence, you probably want to exit the relationship sooner rather than later. Likewise, it is unacceptable to abuse your partner.

1.  Has he ever hit you or raised his fist at you?
2.  Has he ever trapped or restrained you?

3. Has he ever forced himself on you sexually?
4. Has he ever threatened to hurt you?
5. Has he ever threatened to commit suicide, harm you or your family if you leave him?
6. Does he isolate you from your friends and family?
7. Does he limit your access to finances, your mobility and communication with others if you did not comply to his wishes?
8. Does he humiliate you?
9. Do you feel psychologically or physically threatened by your partner?
10. Have you ever hit or pushed your partner?
11. Have you ever pinched him in anger, or pulled his hair?

Some of you have been a victim of physical or psychological abuse but remain unaware. Abusers tend to be manipulative as well. He may convince you that his tough love is right for you; that it is your fault when he misbehaves.

Since you likely love your partner a lot, you will want to believe that he is a good person when he really isn't. You feel comfortable staying with someone who knows you well and whom you think loves you. Stay in an abusive toxic relationship too long, and you will find it difficult to accept and love a truly good man when he comes your way.

## Lessons Learnt

Violence and abuse are simply not acceptable be the victim your partner or you. If you suspect that you are the victim of such abuse, seek help.

# Chapter 17

**Know and accept that men and women are different**
*"A wise woman puts a grain of sugar in everything she says to a man, and takes a grain of salt with everything he says to her." – Helen Rowland*

## Coffee with Sophia

In a conversation with a woman…

*Woman: "I don't get him. We had a miscommunication and I am trying so damn hard to reach out to him but he retreated into his 'man cave'. Not a word. He went silent, he refused to talk about his feelings and I am trying to help him understand how I feel."*

In another conversation with a man…

*Man: "We had a fight and we haven't spoken for a while now. I told her I just need time for myself. I probably just need a couple of weeks to myself, play soccer with friends, go to the gym, focus on work. Maybe I'll reach out to her in a couple of weeks."*
Me: *"A couple of weeks?!!"*

## Thought of the day

Most of us are aware that men and women are different but do we *actually* know how different we are?

Men and women manage stresses and solve problems differently. We have dissimilar interpretations of pride and respect.

How are we different?

1. Stress and conflict management – women prefer to talk while men tend to recluse
2. Dealing with problems – women focuses on the process, men focuses on finding solutions
3. When in pain – women need to be comforted and reassured; men distance themselves and hide away
4. Instinctive attributes – women are nurturing, caring, community-centric, expressive and focus on forming bonds; men are wired to be destructive, armed with killer instinct, have a relatively lower tendency to form bonds and view silence as a form of strength
5. Ego – men are very prideful compared to women
6. Rumination tendency – women are more inclined to ruminate
7. View on sex – women see this as a primary expression of love, care and bonding while men often view sex as meeting a physical need and then, an expression of love, care and bonding.
8. Emotional needs – women have relatively higher emotional needs than men

9.  Need to feel respected – men have much, much, much…much higher need to feel respected
10. Parental instinct – women have strong maternal instincts while men tend to act as protectors of their clans
11. Pain endurance –women have a higher pain endurance
12. Need for space – men generally need more space than women
13. Frequently-used words used to describe women - feeling, warm, intuitive, nurturing, emotional, courageous, enduring, soft, chatty, weak, complex
14. Frequently-used words to describe men - logical, perceptive, judging, objective, brave, problem-solving, hard, strong, aloof, cold, big babies

A man once shared, *"I would rather undertake the task to build a company, than to understand what is going on in a woman's head. You never know from one moment to the next what's going to come flying out of her mouth. Women are too complex!"* We think that men don't get us. But most men feel the same way – that we, women, refuse to understand them too!

Recognize and accept that we are wired differently – the way we think, manage ourselves, express our love, react when in pain, solve problems. Armed with that knowledge, you can then develop some tools and tricks to cope with the gender differences.

**Lessons Learnt**

Why else would twenty-two men go after a ball for ninety minutes, and men from all over the world gather around the tv set to see twenty-two men chase a ball? Box

## Chapter 18

### Avoid attacking him below the belt
*"Hurting people hurt people." – John C. Maxwell*

**Coffee with Sophia**

*"What she said made me seem like less of a man. She can be so unkind when it comes to commenting about my height and my physical attributes. I can't change those! She doesn't respect me and I don't know if I can be with a woman who is constantly emasculating and disrespecting me."*

**Thought of the day**

As a woman, you hold tremendous power over your partner. You can build a man up as much as you can tear him down. Personal attacks launched at a man can be emasculating and some blows are below the belt. You don't want to go there.

1. Short men are conscious of their heights
2. Small, bald or skinny men can be sensitive about their physical appearance.
3. Men are generally sensitive about how well-endowed they are, don't make negative remarks or comparison with other men.
4. His ability to earn
5. How he compares to other men – physical attributes, achievements, finances

6. Though men with receding hairline may sometimes joke about it, it doesn't mean that they will welcome you making fun of that.
7. Physical attributes that he cannot change – his voice, soft jaw line, narrow shoulders, his build

Men desires respect more than anything else from his woman and personal attacks that are below the belt will come across as disrespectful and emasculating. If you find that your partner is particularly sensitive about certain attributes, then avoid the temptation of hurting him where you know it hurts most, especially when you are emotionally charged. You don't want to erode his self-esteem, and hurt his pride and feelings.

**Lessons Learnt**

If a man feels disrespected and emasculated around you, he may look elsewhere for a woman who is able to respects and loves him for who he is.

# Chapter 19

## If you keep a scorecard, don't

*"A spirit to find fault is an enemy to your peace and comfort,*
*and to the happiness of those around you. It is the key to*
*your destruction." - Anonymous*

### Coffee with Sophia

A young man shared his story with me about how his ex had kept a list of her faults over a period of three years. She would start counting his faults over the years each time they got into a fight. He admitted that he could no longer remember the number of times she would make him apologize for the same mistakes. Over time, her scorecard grew and this made him weary and unhappy. He eventually left the relationship.

### Thought of the day

While a good memory can be a blessing, it can also be a curse if you use that gift to keep a scorecard of your partner's blunders. Digging up and entangling the past with current issues can only lead to one thing – a toxic cocktail of mess.

Instead of holding on to grudges, why not count your blessings? Let him know how grateful you are to have met the wonderful man that he is. Give him a chance know that you appreciate his good behaviors and efforts.

None of us are perfect, not you and certainly not I. We want our partner to love us for who we are. We expect him to accept that we are as human as he is and will make mistakes. But can we come to terms with the fact that he too is flawed and can make just as many mistakes? Keeping a scorecard of his slipups is therefore quite unhelpful. Instead of focusing on his mistakes and reinforcing him negatively, why not help him be a better man?

**Lessons Learnt**

Keeping a list of your partner's fault can quickly sour your relationship. Throw the scorecard away, tomorrow is a new day and both of you will have a new opportunity to be better versions of yourselves. A man who loves you can often bring the best out of you, can you bring the best out of him too?

## Chapter 20

### Positive reinforcement works better than constant criticism

*"A person who feels appreciated will do more than what is expected."*

**Coffee with Sophia**

*"You don't make time to call."*
*"I had a dreadful day, why are you being so unsupportive and cold?"*
*"Why don't you ever take the garbage out?"*
*"Why don't you take the lead for a change and organize the trip instead of having me do it all on my own."*
*"Why can't you spend more time with the kids and I?"*

Why don't you this, why don't you that, you are horrible, you are mean, you are selfish, you are inconsiderate, it's all your fault. If a kid constantly hears of how bad, incapable and unintelligent he is, he may grow up into all that one day. Negative reinforcement can be a self-fulfilling prophecy.

**Thought of the day**

Imagine having a partner that criticizes you all the time - your physical appearance, weight, hair, career, behaviors actions. He tells you about how inadequate a partner you are. He complains each time you are late, he gets angry when your bosses make you stay late at work. Though you do your best to keep the house in order, make career sacrifices for him and your children, he does not seem to value that. All he does is criticize, complain and remind you of how bad you are each time you err.

Now, let's admit that we have sometimes made the mistake of repeatedly criticizing our partners. We don't give compliments and our appreciation often enough. B.F. Skinner, an Edgar Pierce Professor of Psychology argued that positive reinforcement is superior to punishment in altering a person's behavior – *'Punishment is not simply the opposite of positive reinforcement; positive reinforcement results in lasting behavioral modification, whereas punishment only temporarily changes behavior and presents many detrimental side effects.'*

Interestingly, according to Harvard, there is an ideal praise-to-criticism ratio in a team – 5.6:1. For every negative criticism that you make, balance it with five or six praises.

1. I love the roses hun, you always put a smile on my face when I feel down. I love you.
2. Thanks for helping me with the shopping bags darling.
3. Thanks for taking the garbage out, that's so sweet of you
4. Thanks for fixing breakfast/lunch/dinner for us, I loved how you prepared the salmon

5. Aww, I love the scent of the coffee you brew every morning, it is so romantic
6. Thanks for being on time hun, *kiss*
7. Thank you for understanding darling
8. Thank you for being honest and open
9. Thank you for always being there to listen
10. I love it when you do this!

So, instead of reminding your partner 24/7 about how bad he is doing, why not compliment him for his good behaviors and when he does things right by you?

**Lessons Learnt**

We all love being rewarded with love, appreciation and money for our efforts and achievements. Using positive reinforcement can result in better behavior alteration in comparison to negative reinforcement. Why not give that a try and see what happens?

# Chapter 21

## Save for rainy days
*"The lack of money is the root of all evil." – Mark Twain*

**Coffee with Sophia**

A friend shared about how her partner left her when the going got tough even though she had supported him through his unemployment.

*"I supported him when he was jobless. I also paid for his graduate degree. I stopped shopping for myself altogether to make sure that we had enough for the apartment rental and our daily expenses. A year after he had graduated, I got laid off from my firm. He was supportive for the first two months."*

*"I had very little savings left and had just enough to last me through the six months of being unemployed. He managed to get a decent paying job after he got his degree. Instead of helping with our expenses, he bought himself a four-thousand-dollar guitar and expensive shirts."*

*"Four months after I got laid off, he left. The months that followed were dark. I got a job after two months after that but I will never forget how I gave all I had to support him financially for three years and he disappeared as soon as it wasn't convenient for him to stay with me."*

**Thought of the day**

Money problem is one of the topmost cited reasons for divorces.

Financial stresses have caused many couples to fight – wedding, holiday, household expenses. As living costs increase, a single income family will find itself financially stretched.

The situation worsens when the breadwinner loses his job or falls ill. The couple may also have parental or child support obligations. The lack of savings can be so stressful that couples break up because of the financial stress.

Below, a list of cashflow surprises people encounter:

1. Retrenchment and prolonged unemployment
2. Unplanned pregnancy
3. Terminal illnesses and chronic medical conditions
4. Setting up a family
5. Buying a new car
6. Expenses for children – education, diapers, food, breastfeeding pumps, childcare, medical expenses
7. Further education
8. Tuition Debt
9. Insurance
10. Vacations
11. Parental or family financial support
12. Bills
13. Robbery, thefts of uninsured large expensive items

14. Mortgage payment or fluctuation in interest rates
15. Need for urgent costly surgeries and medical care

As you plan your future with your partner, it will be wise to think about having sufficient funds to meet your needs. Then comes the discipline to prioritize your spending, make investments, execute your plans and sign up for appropriate insurance plans.

**Lessons Learnt**

Money problems have destroyed many marriages. It can be very stressful to lose your job, fall sick and have large cashflow needs at the same time. Save for rainy days, you never know when it may rain or how long the monsoon will last when it hits.

# Chapter 22

## Men are visual creatures, look and stay physically attractive

*"Men are visually aroused by women's bodies and less sensitive to their arousal by women's personalities because they are trained early into that response."* – Naomi Wolf

### Coffee with Sophia

A gentleman once shared very candidly that looks were just as important as brains.

*"We are wired to be visual. All else being equal, it will only make sense for us to go after a more beautiful woman. Wouldn't you do the same? You fall in love with words, we fall in love with what we see. We can be shallow like that."*

### Thought of the day

Men are visual creatures and likes his partner to look aesthetically pleasing.

Anyone can be a beautiful siren, it is a matter of taking the time and making the effort to be one.

Occasionally, we hear of or know of a woman who has let herself go after she has settled down. She used to be gorgeous – flawless skin, perfectly-shaped body, beautiful hair. It can be quite a shame indeed!

As women age, it can be worthwhile to pay attention to staying in shape and to maintaining your health. Cultivating a good lifestyle, diet and exercise habits can help you achieve that.

1. Go to bed early, get enough sleep – this helps maintain a youthful and fresh complexion, sharp mind and can prevent dark eye circles. Ah, these eye bags.
2. Drink 8 glasses of water daily.
3. Exercise – cardio exercises to lose weight such as brisk walking, cycling, running or swimming; yoga and mild resistance training to keep your body toned.
4. Health supplement – multi-vitamins to maintain your overall wellbeing, Vitamin C as anti-oxidant, Vitamin E and collagen supplements for your hair and skin, Glucosamine and calcium for joints, bone and teeth health, iron supplement for post-menstrual anemic tendencies, fish oil to maintain a healthy brain.
5. Healthy food choices – generous intakes of fruits and vegetables, olive oil for cooking, moderate red meat intake, fresh and unprocessed food whenever possible, moderate health and sugar intake, dark chocolate in moderation, whole grains, nuts, moderate caffeine intake (yup, apparently research has shown that it may help lower risk of some

cancers, Parkinson's disease, Type 2 diabetes and provide some level of DNA damage?).

6. Moderate your alcohol intake if you must drink.
7. Manage your stress level – go for a spa, hit the gym, go for a walk, talk to your girlfriends, don't bottle things up
8. Maintain your general and oral hygiene.
9. Maintain a healthy weight.
10. Basic grooming of hair and nails.

Take your time to enjoy the process of dressing up and looking beautiful not only for men but for yourself. You will feel better about yourself, be more confident and have a more positive outlook on your day too!

**Lessons Learnt**

Men are visual creatures. Look and stay physically attractive not only for them, but for yourself!

# Chapter 23

## Respect him

*"Women need love and men need respect." – Emerson Eggerichs*

**Coffee with Sophia**

*"I don't get why he sometimes say that I do not respect him. Trivial comments can spark that off – career, other men, his friends, his choice of shirt. Sometimes, when I disagree with him, he found me disrespectful. Where do I stop? On the one hand, I want us to be honest with each other, and on the other hand, he feels that I distrust him. That somewhat equates to me not respecting him."*

**Thought of the day**

Many men had commented that they cannot be a woman who cannot respect them, even if she is madly in love with him. So, do men really need to feel that he is respected more than he is loved by his partner?

When does a man think you disrespect him?

1. When you distrust him
2. When you question his judgement
3. When you embarrass him in public
4. When you indicate that his ability to earn is inferior

5. When you make him feel that his professional, problem-solving or logical abilities are subpar
6. If he finds out that you have spoken ill of him when you shared your relationship issues with friends and family
7. When you communicate disrespect – turning your back at him when he speaks, replying with harsh tones, belittling him, dismissing his opinion or advice
8. When you make him feel like he is a failure
9. Do you defend him if he is humiliated by his friends or family?

It can be helpful to let your partner know explicitly that you respect his judgement and abilities. Thanking him for his help and advice makes him feel respected. And when he asks for you to trust him, show him that you have faith in him.

**Lessons Learnt**

Respect is very important to a man. Know your boundaries to avoid disrespecting him unintentionally.

# Chapter 24

## Stop judging him, love him

*"It's the umm…the Roman God, Janus. My mother gave it to me when I was little. She wanted to teach me that people have two sides. A good side, a bad side, a past, a future. And that we must embrace both in someone we love." –
Angelina Jolie in the Tourist*

### Coffee with Sophia

*"Do not judge your partner, but rather, love him. Nurture the boy and respect the man in him. Remember, even the most tempting rose, will have thorns. You need to embrace your differences and accept that you deal with things uniquely. Like you, he is flawed. It will take a lifetime of patience, mutual acceptance and unconditional love to help each other become better people. Judging him won't help. It will only hurt him and your relationship."*

*"You need to understand that your partner grew up in a different family and parental upbringing. He could have been from a different country, cultural background and age group. There may be many dissimilarities between the both of you - values, how you view the world, how you manage challenges, your take on finances, how you want to bring up your children…the list goes on. Embrace these differences and don't judge him because judging will undermine your relationship. Love him for who he is."*

**Thought of the day**

Every day, we judge - the woman walking down the street, how our colleagues are dressed, the man with spilt coffee on his shirt at the subway, the person standing in line ordering her coffee, the receptionist when she greets us, how the waitresses are dressed at a restaurant and how our bosses behave.

If your partner feels that you are constantly judging him, he may start to feel as if you don't appreciate him for who he is. He will feel inadequate as he cannot live up to your expectations. He will begin to wonder if he is able to make you happy at all and will be convinced that you are better off with someone else - a man who is good enough, has what you want and behaves in a way you like.

The more you judge him, the more he will think that you do not love him anymore. Love him, don't judge him.

**Lessons Learnt**

Everyone has flaws and rough edges that need polishing. Instead of judging your partner, you can try loving him for who he is and focus on bringing out the best in him.

# Chapter 25

**Have your own circle of friends and let him have his**
*"Friendship is unnecessary, like philosophy, like art...It has no survival value; rather it is one of those things that give value to survival." – C.S. Lewis*

## Coffee with Sophia

*"I've been so busy that I was unable to stay in touch with my girlfriends. I didn't realize that I became overly dependent on him to be my everything – to listen to all my complaints, be there for my when I'm sad and to lift me up. He started to describe me as being clingy and needy, I felt very bad about myself. Took me a while to reconnect with my friends and lucky for me, I now have my own emotional and social support network."*

## Thought of the day

You were love-struck and you designed your life around him. You have gradually isolated yourself from friends and family without realizing that you are doing it. All is good until one day, your partner can no longer manage your emotional demands.

You've grown to be unhealthily codependent on your partner. Codependency is when one has excessive emotional or psychological reliance on a partner. This person typically has some form of illness or addiction and requires support.

Sometimes, a partner who is immature, has poor self-esteem or lack achievements may be at risk of developing codependency.

Having your own circle of friends gives you space to develop as individuals. As there's always a limit as to how much a person can listen and support you, girlfriends can come in quite handy. Don't risk overloading your partner with your daily venting and emotional venting. As an alternative, call your girlfriends and go party with them.

**Lessons Learnt**

Do maintain your circle of good and trustworthy girlfriends. Also, give your partner his space to be with his friends.

# Chapter 26

## Double standards - put yourself in his shoes
*"For the powerful, crimes are those that others commit." –*
*Noam Chomsky*

## Coffee with Sophia

*"Don't you see it? It's always about you - how you feel,*
*what you need, what you want. What about how I feel, what*
*I need and what I want? You give me a hard time when I*
*spend time with my friends, my family. You kick a fuss when*
*I am the one pulling my hours in the office. We have to plan*
*our life around your schedule. When I ask for a compromise*
*and for you to meet me half way, you think that*
*unreasonable. Don't you see that there's some double*
*standard going on here?"*

## Thought of the day

Every now and then, you get bogged down by the things
that you must do to make a living, your troubles, your
emotions and your needs. Your experience of the world will
seem more real, feelings more intense and stresses heavier
than that of any the other persons.

We forget that our partner can feel as much pain as we do.
He too can feel fatigued after a day of arduous work,
despaired when met with relationship disappointments,
heartbreak when you say hurtful and insecure when lacking

affirmation. We forget to put ourselves in his shoes and see the world through his eyes. We feel entitled to being treated more fairly and that our happiness comes first.

Do you have double standard in your relationship?

1. Have you been accused of having double standard?
2. Do you feel that it is ok for you to spend time with your friends but not he?
3. Do you feel that you are entitled to your privacy but it is acceptable to violate his – checking his letters, his mobile, emails, journal, files in his computer?
4. Do you feel that it is ok for you to have drinks or meals with male counterparts but it is not if your partner does the same?
5. Have you often blamed your partner for your relationship problems but failed to see your part in solving them?
6. Do you have a strong sense of entitlement general?

Is there a double standard in any of these areas in your relationship?

1. Shared finances – do you want sole control?
2. Spending – do you criticize the way he spends but expect that he respects your spending habits?
3. Time with family and friends – do you find yourself asking him to be home when he has a night out with his friends but expect that he lets you party all night
4. Privacy – do you intrude into his privacy but expect yours to be respected?

5. Time – do you demand punctuality of him but you are often late or cancel last minute?
6. Emotions – is his emotions as important as yours?
7. Trust – do you question his loyalty and love constantly but expects that he fully trusts you
8. Household chores – do you demand that he does more than his share?

It is unfair to hold your partner to a strict set of standard but excuse yourself of the same. He will end up resenting you. Having a double standard can sabotage your relationship in the long run.

**Lessons Learnt**

Your partner appreciates fairness in expectation and treatment as much as you do. Put yourself in his shoes often and avoid having double standard in your relationship.

# Chapter 27

**The four pillars – love, trust, respect, honesty**

*"In a relationship, honesty and trust must exist. If they don't, there's no point of loving. So if you can't afford to be honest, stay single." – Anonymous*

## Coffee with Sophia

*"What makes a good relationship?"* I asked my sister who has been blissfully married for fifteen years.

*"As far as I am concerned, there are four important pillars in a relationship – love, trust, respect and honesty."* She answered with strong conviction.

*"You see that on our wall? Love is patient, love is kind. It does not envy, it does not boast, it is not proud. It does not dishonor others, it is not self-seeking, it is not easily angered. It keeps no record of wrongs. Love does not delight in evil but rejoices with the truth. Love always protects, always trusts, always hopes, always perseveres."*

## Thought of the day

*"The second pillar is trust – the confidence that your partner has placed in you and you him. It is a duty of a wife, to protect her husband's trust. What you do when he isn't around, the choices that you make for your family and children. Never do anything to break that trust because*

*once broken, it will never be the same again. The same goes for your trust in him. Have faith in him and you will save yourselves from many fights that stem from distrust."*

*"The third – respect. Respect is particularly important for men as they seem to put that above many other things in life. A man wants to be respected for his abilities, judgment and character; a sort of non-opinionated due regard to your partner."*

*"The final one – honesty. Do not lie to your partner, the minute you start having secrets, you will start telling one lie to cover another lie. Don't go there."*

## Lessons Learnt

*"These four pillars – love, trust, respect and honesty, can be a stronghold in your relationship. Guard these closely and you should be okay."*

# Chapter 28

## Give and take

*"Marriage is an empty box. It remains empty unless you put in more than you take out." – John C. Maxwell*

**Coffee with Sophia**

*"I'm so tired of giving. I'm expected to give in to her emotional needs, follow her schedule, provide for her and be strong for her. I am expected to be understanding when she has a difficult day at work. I'm expected to go out of my way for her comfort. A healthy relationship needs to be one with both partners giving and taking. I'm exhausted and I don't think I can go on giving without getting anything in return. At some point, I need to love myself."*

**Thought of the day**

Some people are great at taking, others at receiving. Keeping a balance of giving and receiving in a relationship is where it gets tricky.

You will have different preferences in the kind of food, movies, friends, activities, music or vacation spots that you like. Being able to compromise and meet your partner half way will be important to keep you happy in the relationship.

1. Does your partner complain about how he's always the one giving?
2. Does he explicitly say that you are selfish?
3. Do you only want things done your way?

4. Do you reciprocate his gestures?
5. Do you give him the silent treatment when he does not give in to you?
6. Do you kick a big fuss when you don't get your way?
7. Are you very independent and find it difficult to receive from your partner?
8. Do you resent your partner for not conceding?
9. Is there something that you can do differently to strike a healthy balance of giving and taking in the relationship?

Show your appreciation when he compromises. Give with a cheerful heart without demanding that he reciprocates. Don't give if you will be resentful later.

**Lessons Learnt**

A relationship forms when two unique individuals with independent set of preferences come together. Learn to give, learn to take and learn to compromise.

## Chapter 29

**Learn to apologize, do not repeat your mistakes**
*"Repentance means unlearning all the self-conceit and self-will that we have been training ourselves into. It means killing part of yourself, undergoing a kind of death." – C.S. Lewis*

### Coffee with Sophia

*"I appreciate that you apologize each time you make a mistake but if you repeat the mistakes all the time, you can't blame me for thinking that you don't mean it when you apologize."*

### Thought of the day

Saying 'I'm sorry' doesn't come naturally to some people. In fact, when they err, they not only refuse to apologize but also, point fingers at others. There are also some who will apologize quickly but continually repeat their mistakes. This makes the apology meaningless.

A few things which we be mindful of:

1. Be the first to apologize – Saying *'I'm really sorry that we fought'* can help soften a fight
2. Mean it when you say you are sorry
3. Avoid repeating your mistakes

4.  Do not bring up the same issues that your partner has already apologized for

At times, you will feel too prideful or hurt to say you are sorry. But, it's never too late to ask for forgiveness even when it feels like that's the last thing you want to do. We all have to start somewhere.

## Lessons Learnt

It doesn't hurt to be the first to apologize. Mean your apology, don't repeat the same mistakes.

## Chapter 30

### Give him a stable home to come home to
*"There is nothing nobler or more admirable than when two people who see eye to eye keep house as man and wife, confounding their enemies and delighting their friends."* –
*Homer*

**Coffee with Sophia**

*"I haven't seen you for months, how have you been?"*

*"Well, I've seen better days? It's been a hell hole at home. She's been unhappy and we fight a lot. You know how demanding my work is. Every day when I get home, she will start. I could hardly take a break or rest. It's been tiring."*

**Thought of the day**

It's been said that a stable home is key to strengthening a man's spirit, confidence and focus at work.

Compare two men who walk into your workplace every day. The first guy has a loving, loyal and supportive wife. She creates a safe and comforting home when he returns daily from work to recharge. They have a healthy sex life, she encourages him to pursue his career ambitions and shows empathy and compassion when he shares his work stresses with her.

Now, let's go to the other guy. His partner often picks a fight with him when he gets home. She fights with him through the night and he gets only three or four hours of sleep at night. He wakes up to an unhappy partner, lacks sleep and rushes to work without breakfast. He feels physically and mentally drained as his partner constantly threatens to walk out on him.

Both men are then tasked with dealing with complex projects, difficult clients and tight deadlines. To top that off, they each face competitive colleagues, demanding bosses and long daily commutes. Which man do you will do better in both his career and personal life? Whom do you think will likely make a mistake on an excel sheet at work?

A distracted man who makes mistakes and underperform at work is likely to get fired.

A supportive partner and stable love life can give you both the strength and mental focus needed to do well at work. Behind every successful man, is a woman. A cliché indeed but nevertheless, one with much truth.

**Lessons Learnt**

The lack of stability in love and at home can emotionally destabilize your partner. Learning to support each other through adversity is important. Be an anchor and a source of stable emotional support to him, he will love you for it.

# Chapter 31

## Put yourself in his shoes

*"Compassion is not a relationship between the healer and the wounded. It's a relationship between equals. Only when we know our own darkness well, can we be present with the darkness of others. Compassion becomes real when we recognize our shared humanity." – Pema Chödrön*

**Coffee with Sophia**

He pulled the car into the garage. It's been a long week and he's gotten only three hours of sleep the past few days. He had promised his wife a nice dinner date that evening but he was exhausted.

*"Sorry honey, I'm really tired today, can we do this next week?"*

**Thought of the day**

Empathy.

The ability and willingness to put ourselves in our partner's shoes when things go wrong is a rare combination. Most conflicts happen when we don't see eye to eye with our partner. We take on the position of defending our own interest and our partner will almost automatically assume the opposite position to defend his interest. This worsens when you are both stressed and tired.

When you don't take time to understand your partner's perspectives and feelings, you tend to make the mistake of assuming the worst of him. You overlook the difference between bad intentions and misguided ones; and you forget about your mutual interest –to love each other and to be happy together.

If you can bring yourself to step into his shoes, you can almost become an extension of him – feeling what he feels, understanding his need for rest, space or time, and showing the empathy that he desperately needs.

Once you are willing to understand and see where he is coming from, you will then be able to scratch beyond the rusty surface of his behavior. When that happens, you will find that it becomes easier to cut him some slack, comfort him and forgive him; and be more willing to work things out together.

**Lessons Learnt**

Put yourself in his shoes, show empathy, compassion and love.

# Chapter 32

## Intimacy – keep the flames alive
*"It is not sex that gives the pleasure, but the lover." –*
*Source*

**Coffee with Sophia**

*"The London School of Economics and Political Science,
LSE, had launch an app to map the happiness of people
across time and space. Which activity do you think tops the
list of making a person happy?"*

*"Sex!"* Shouted a male student from Denmark, cheekily.

*"How did 'work' fare in this study? For those of you who
had paid over a hundred and fifty thousand dollars for an
Ivy League MBA to spend more time at work, I have news
for you!"*

The professor turned to the next slide with the results of the
study. The class roared.

**Thought of the day**

Yep, sex topped the list.

You must be curious about the results that LSE had done on
activities that make us happiest and least happy.

Index of pleasure:

1. Intimacy, making love 14.2
2. Theatre, dance, concert 9.3
3. Exhibition, museum, library 8.8
4. Sports, exercise 8.1
5. Gardening, allotment 7.8
6. Singing, performing 6.9
7. Talking, chatting, socializing 6.4
8. Nature watching 6.3
9. Walking, hiking 6.2
10. Hunting, fishing 5.8
11. Drinking alcohol 5.7
12. Hobbies, arts, crafts 5.5
13. Meditating, religious activities 4.9
14. Sports event 4.4
15. Childcare, playing with children 4.1
26. Reading 1.5
27. Listening to a speech, podcast 1.4
28. Washing, dressing, grooming 1.2
29. Sleeping, resting, relaxing 1.1
30. Smoking 0.7
31. Browsing the net 0.6
32. Texting, email, social media 0.6
33. Housework, chores, DIY -0.7
34. Traveling, commuting -1.5
35. In a meeting, seminar, class -1.5
36. Admin, finances, organizing -2.5
37. Waiting, queuing -3.5
38. Care or help for adults -4.3
39. Work, studying -5.4

40. Sick in bed -20.4

(Source: Mappiness/Centre for Economic Performance at the LSE)

A lot of couples have been so tied up with work that they no longer take time out to have sex. How much sex you need will vary from how much your partner needs. Does he need sex once a week, twice a week or daily? Finding that out can prevent the relationship from ending up with one partner feeling sexually deprived. Sexual deprivation in a relationship can send a guy in search of a third party to meet his needs.

It is probably worthwhile for you to learn about your partner's sexual needs, know his preferences in bed and make time for intimacy every week. Keeping the flames alive in your relationship can be a good way to increase your index of happiness as a couple.

**Lessons Learnt**

Keep the flame alive!

# Chapter 33

## Support and inspire him

*"We make a living by what we get, we make a life by what we give." – Winston Churchill*

### Coffee with Sophia

*"Sometimes, I'm too tired to give my husband the emotional support he needs. He told me the other day that he was worried about his job. His company got acquired and there's been another wave of redundancy. Apparently, an entire department got removed last week. I dismissed his concern and said that there was nothing to be worried about. He was so disappointed that I wasn't supportive and said that I had totally dampened his spirit. Now, he doesn't even want to speak to me about it anymore. I feel really bad."*

### Thought of the day

*'A successful man is a man who can earn more than what a woman can spend. And a successful woman is one who can find that man!'*

What they don't say is that the woman is often a strong source of strength and inspiration to cheer him on. Indeed, behind every successful a man is often a woman. But, even the most successful and strongest men will fall every now and then. A supportive partner will reach down to pull him up, provide comfort and inspire him do better.

It is also said that, *'An ideal husband is someone with an ideal wife; and that an ideal wife is someone with an ideal husband.'*

1. Do you know what your partner's dreams are?
2. What does he need to achieve his goals?
3. How do you show or communicate your support to him?
4. What do you do when he is defeated?
5. Do you encourage him to pursue the things that make him happy?
6. What are the three things that you can do this week to better inspire and support him?
7. What are the three things that have been bogging him down that you can stop doing?

Take good care of him as he will also take good care of you.

**Lessons Learnt**

Support and inspire your partner especially when the going gets tough. Bring out the best in him and have faith in the man you have chosen to spend your life with.

## Chapter 34

**Be the change you want to see in your relationship**
*"Success in a marriage does not come merely through finding the right mate, but through being the right mate." –*
*Barnett Brickner*

### Coffee with Sophia

*"It isn't about managing your partner, or changing your partner but more so, managing yourself. The question is, do you love him enough, to be the change you want to see in your relationship?"*

### Thought of the day

If you take a closer look at your relationship, some of the frictions that you have had in your relationship may have been due to old habits and unresolved issues. Getting rid of old habits, behaviors and reactions can be counter-intuitive. On the one hand, you are now wiser because of the lessons that you've learnt in the past. But on the other hand, if you aren't careful, these very lessons can form groundless fears, crystallize bad reactions and become barriers that will sabotage your relationships.

How do you balance the need to change and the need to assert healthy boundaries at the same time? There is no easy answer to this and each relationship will have a unique answer.

Being self-aware, can be the first few steps in identifying the areas of improvement in our relationship. Then, we can figure out what needs to be done differently. It will be challenging to face up to our own flaws and weaknesses as the truth can sometimes be ugly.

1. What are the top three changes that you want to see in your relationship?
2. Do you often contribute to the solution or do you have a habit of worsening a problem?
3. What are the three things that you can start doing to improve your relationship?
4. What are the three things that you can keep doing to maintain a healthy relationship?
5. What are the three things that you need to stop doing to prevent your relationship from declining?

Doing nothing is easy and that's why so many people choose to do nothing. It will take courage and strength as you take your first steps to being that change you want to see in your relationship.

**Lessons Learnt**

You are either the problem or the solution. Staying on the fence or being passive when there's only two of you, will mean that you are still part of the problem. If you want to see changes in your relationship, how about being that change and see what happens?

# Chapter 35

## Understand him more, love him less

*"Men wake up aroused in the morning. We can't help it. We just wake up and we want you. And the women are thinking – how can he want me the way I look in the morning? It's because we can't see you. We have no blood anywhere near our optic nerve." – Rooney*

### Coffee with Sophia

*What is he doing now? How can I make him happier? What do I need to do, so that he can love me more? How often should I text or call him? Why is he spending time with his friends and not me? Does he still love me?*

You get all tangled up in your head with questions and start concocting stories that don't exist. Yes, he loves you. But if you keep badgering him, he will have start to have issues with you.

### Thought of the day

A woman tends to give her heart to a man quickly, fall in love deeply and forget that it may serve her well to instead love him a little lesser and understand him a lot more.

A woman in love will want to spend all her time with her partner - shower him with love, share her happiness and sadness with him. She gets so intense that she makes him feel pressured and suffocated. He becomes overwhelmed and begins to pull away. The more he withdraws, the more she reaches out to him.

However, if she puts in effort to understand a man, she will learn that he needs time and space to recover after a long day of work. He needs to spend time with his friends to be the boy that he is inside.

Men appreciate the opportunity to chase women. They love the hunt and prize those that are difficult to get. Sometimes, letting him be so that he has a chance to miss you is more effective than giving him a deluge of romantic gestures.

**Lessons Learnt**

Love him less, let him be and understand him more. You can save yourself from a lot of heartache in the long run.

# Chapter 36

## Mindfulness – take time to enjoy your relationship
*"Many of us made our world so familiar that we do not see it anymore." – Anam Cara*

### Coffee with Sophia

*"We become so busy with our work and preoccupied with checking off our to-do list including learning how to be the person we want to become that we forget to live in the present. Our children playing in the living room and our husbands watching tv are simply another set of fixtures in the house as we power up the laptop to work after a day of labor in the office. We let our life pass us by when we forget to practice mindfulness and make time to enjoy our relationships and family. We forget about being a woman."*

### Thought of the day

You are obsessed with going after the next promotion, hunting for the next big role and collecting yet another piece of degree. You reminisce your past romance, ruminate over your mistakes and get hung up with what could have been if you had done things differently. You waltz into your house with the autopilot mode on, peck your husband on his cheek and hug your children.

With your mind elsewhere, you do not see the twinkle in his eyes nor feel the love of his embrace. You do not hear the excitement in your children's voice as they show you the medal that they have won in school today. You are so desperate to be the person you can be tomorrow that you stop living in the present.

Are you guilty of not practicing mindfulness in your daily lives? Do you take time to enjoy your relationship? Are you truly present when you spend time with your partner and children?

Tadeusz Różewicz, a polish writer shared that, *"It is more difficult to spend a day well than to write a book."*

**Lessons Learnt**

Mindfulness – take time to enjoy your relationship. Celebrate little wins and milestones with your partner and your children. Be conscious of the present moment. Don't wake up tomorrow and find yourself asking yourself, *"What happened to yesterday?"*

## Chapter 37

### Stay positive, joyful and happy

*"I think happiness is what makes you pretty. Period. Happy people are beautiful." – Drew Barrymore*

### Coffee with Sophia

*"I'm sorry that I wasn't able to be there with you. I've had a lot to deal with lately. You may not have been aware of this, but you harbor a lot of negativity. This drags people around you down. During our conversations, you often directed so much negative energy at me that I feel mentally drained and physically exhausted after hanging out with you."*

### Thought of the day

Constant negativity from a partner can drag the other one down and ruin a relationship.

Taking yourself less seriously and simply choosing to stay positive, joyful and happy can lift both your spirits every day. Of course, there are times when you need to have that serious conversation. You can actually change the course of your discussion and positively affect the outcome by staying optimistic and by framing the issues in a constructive manner.

Be care not to make conversations heavier than they ought to be, or give a problem more weight than it deserves. We hear a lot about how men dislike drama and girlfriends that complain, nag or cry a little too often. I'm sure we don't want to be that.

An infectious laughter can soften your partner's heart more effectively than a harsh or negative tone. The positive energy that you create in your relationship will help you resolve your conflicts better and allow the two of you to feel more relaxed in each other's company.

**Lessons Learnt**

Staying cheerful and delighting in your partner's presence can affect your relationship positively. Take it easy, stay positive, joyful and happy.

# Chapter 38

## Don't take him for granted

*"Don't take me for granted. Because, unlike others, I am not afraid to walk away." – Anonymous*

### Coffee with Sophia

*"This is what I think - the more I make time for her and tell her that I love her, the more she takes me for granted. She stopped thanking me when I go out of my way to do nice things for her. She had even started to expect that of me. Even though I try to make her feel special, she doesn't do the same for me. I don't want to sound weak but she makes me feel unwanted and unappreciated."*

### Thought of the day

Do you take your partner for granted? When you have been together for a while, you forget how much you have gone through to meet this special person in your life.

He goes out of his way to make you feel special and he does little things daily to show you that he loves you. The more secure you feel, the more you start to take him for granted. You start to become complacent because you know that he will not walk away from you. You are so used to him loving you unconditionally that you only receive, and not give.

Don't take him for granted.

1. Tell him that you love him
2. Thank him when he goes out of his way to make you happy
3. Reciprocate his romantic gestures
4. Every now and then, do things to make him feel special
5. Remind yourself not to fall into the trap of overfamiliarity

That said, do also make sure that you do not put yourself in the position of being taken for granted. It sure is important to put him first every now and then but don't give him the idea that it is okay to put you in the position of being second permanently.

**Lessons Learnt**

Cherish him and don't take him for granted.

# Chapter 39

## Have courage amidst crisis

*"Lots of people want to ride with you in the limo, but what you want is someone who will take the bus with you when the limo breaks down." – Oprah Winfrey*

### Coffee with Sophia

*"This is my first pregnancy. I've been feeling out of sorts lately; my belly button has popped and I am thirty-two weeks pregnant. My husband has just lost his job and we took a mortgage last year. I think we are in a crisis."*

### Thought of the day

As women, we are expected to climb the corporate ladder, go through a pregnancy and be sidelined for a promotion just because we can't join the boys in the bathroom, or at the gentlemen clubs. We are expected to keep our family fed, do well at work, keep the house clean, babysit the kids and be a slut in the bedroom. If any two or more of these pieces crumble concurrently, we may very quickly sink into a crisis.

When things seem like they are falling apart, take courage.

1. Remind yourself that it too shall past
2. Stay positive

3. Change the things that you can change, accept the things that you can't and have the wisdom to know the difference
4. Don't quit
5. Avoid being hasty in making big life decisions in times of crisis
6. Do not ruminate over things that you cannot change
7. Be resilient

There are many things that can put your relationship into an emergency mode. But do know that none of us are immune to that; a crisis can strike anytime to any of us. Some common challenges:

1. One or both of you experience redundancy at work
2. Pregnancy complications
3. Motor vehicle accidents
4. Incapacitating medical conditions that lead to short- or medium-term intensive care requirements
5. Addictions
6. Post-natal depression
7. Death of a family member, children
8. Midlife crisis
9. Excessive intervention by in-laws
10. Sudden loss of wealth
11. Excess workplace stresses

If your partner is going through a crisis, the pressure can be tremendously testing. He will need your support and encouragement. Be courageous and stick together as a team.

Your relationship will grow stronger after the snowstorm is over.

**Lessons Learnt**

We will all experience at least a crisis or two in our relationship. Being a good-weathered partner is easy. The true test to a relationship is when you go through a crisis together – do you take courage, stick together and support each other during challenging times?

# Chapter 40

*Avoid.*

## Withholding sex, love and affection

*"Withholding sex, love or affection is psychological manipulation and abuse."*

*Add man's background.*

### Coffee with Sophia

*"Whenever she didn't get her way, she would withhold sex. She would turn her back when we sleep, withhold her affections and punish me until she got what she wanted. I was very unhappy and imagined how life would be if we got married. At the end, I called our engagement off."*

### Thought of the day

*① manipulate / tool*

*Some women use sex, love & affection w/ power to gain*

Withholding sex, love or affection in your relationship can cause your partner to grow distant and feel inadequate. He will feel sexually dissatisfied and may eventually leave the relationship or turn to someone else.

1. Do you withhold sex in your relationship?
2. Do you distant yourself and refuse to have physical contact with your partner if he angers you?
3. Do you deprive him of affection when he doesn't give in to you?

~~Withholding sex from your partner can cause him to feel less close to you over time.~~ A woman sometimes has the power to make her partner do things that she wants by withholding love, sex or affection from him. But this doesn't mean that it is healthy. In fact, in the long run, the fate of the relationship is questionable.

## Lessons Learnt

Avoid the temptation of withholding sex, love or affection from your partner to be in the position of power and control, because, you may lose him.

## Chapter 41

### Avoid falling into a routine

*"If you think adventure is dangerous, try routine, it is lethal." – Paul Coelho*

**Coffee with Sophia**

*"People ask me what's my secret to keeping my marriage happy. I'm thirty-nine. My husband and I were high-school sweet hearts. We have three children, and we've been married for seventeen years,"* she giggled.

*"I always tell people that it's easy to fall into a routine – waking up, prepping the kids, getting ready for work, taking them to school and rushing to work. Routine takes away the excitement and fun in relationships. We are cognizant of that and make conscious efforts to try different restaurants and arrange babysitters so that we continue to go for our weekly dates. We pick different travel locations and explore new things in the bedroom. You've got to keep creating pleasant surprises and not let your relationship fall into a routine."*

**Thought of the day**

Do you make conscious efforts to keep your relationship exciting and fun? Do you occasionally surprise your partner with things that he likes?

It's very easy for couples to follow a routine after some time. On the one hand, a routine provides for a predictable schedule but on the other hand, routines can cause a sense of repetition. Over time, the couple may be tempted to look for excitement elsewhere as boredom sets in.

How do you avoid falling into a routine in your relationship?

1. Strive to create surprises for your partner
2. Pick a new restaurant to go to every few weeks
3. Avoid cooking or ordering in the same kinds of food
4. Learn something new together
5. Explore unusual places when you go on vacation
6. Spend time with different sets of friends every now and then
7. Go on romantic dates as you did when you first met

**Lessons Learnt**

Don't fall into a routine as your relationship develops. Find new things to do, create surprises and enjoy new experiences together. Spice up your relationship regularly so that your days won't be repetitive and dull.

# Chapter 42

## In-laws, build your bridges, maintain your boundaries

*"Did you realize that when you married your Prince or Princess Charming, you inherited the king, the queen and the whole court?" – Dr David Stoop and Dr Jan Stoop*

### Coffee with Sophia

*"I have been very welcoming to my in-laws when they came to my home, or well, at least I thought so. His brother and sister were sometimes here with their partners. I would give them a set of keys and ask them to feel at home. We moved into a new apartment and my mother-in-law stayed over. The first thing that she did was to tell me how the ironing board was inadequate. She then went on to complain about the laundry, choice of toilet bleaches, dish washing liquid and how I ran my household. She was relentless."*

### Thought of the day

Not all the in-laws understand that they are actually guests in your house and that they should follow your rules, just as they would expect you to when you are a guest at theirs.

In-laws can be a tricky business. I have heard of many couples with supportive in-laws that go out of their way to support them. Some in-laws would go the extra mile to take their grandchildren to school and extra-curricular activities.

That said, I have also heard of in-laws who incessantly judge and make life a living hell for the married couple.

It may seem daunting initially, the idea of building bridges with your in-laws. They can be your biggest pain or biggest ally. Hopefully they become the latter.

Make time to get to know them, see them as people and assume the best of them. Understand that there is a bond between your husband and his mother just like the one that you will form with your son. It will serve you well to work with your partner to manage them, respect their boundaries and maintain yours. Similarly, help your partner build bridges with your family.

*"Two men were in the pub. One says to his mate – 'My mother-in-law is an angel.' His friend replies, 'you're lucky. Mine is still alive.'."*

Though it can sometimes feel that way, it really can't be that bad, I mean…

**Lessons Learnt**

In-laws can either be a boon or a bane to your relationship. It can be worthwhile investing time, effort and care to build a good rapport with them. It can get rocky at times but as we all know, when you bring two families together, you can sometimes get one hell of a circus.

# Chapter 43

## The little ones – make time for them

*"If you want your children to turn out well, spend twice as much time with them, and half as much money." – Abigail Van Burren*

## Coffee with Sophia

*"I know this sounds cheesy but I will say it anyway. It was when I first held her in my arms that I realized the meaning of life. It has been challenging to balance my schedule as a C-level executive in a pharmaceutical company but parenting is a privilege A child's upbringing will influence her mannerism, her sense of self-worth, her resilience, and how she carries herself. One day, I will become a memory to my little girl but to do that, I must first give her that memory."*

## Thought of the day

We get so busy seeking power and making money that we sometimes forget that being parents means that we have a duty to parent our children.

Indeed, being parents entails parenting children.

It is said that a child's mind benefits much from quality engagement early in life. Activities and conversations that engage the child's mind and stimulate his curiosities will inspire a child to learn.

Your little ones may be a part of your world, but you are their entire world, especially when they are young.

1. Do you make time for your children?
2. Do you listen to them when they reach out to you with questions?
3. Do you pay attention to them when they share their thoughts with you?
4. Do you take time out to play with them?
5. Are you spending too much time at the office?
6. Do you think that you neglect your children often?
7. Do you lose your patience with them often?

A child is like a blank canvas that you can create a masterpiece of. He needs your careful guidance as he learns about the world, good manners and good behaviors. You will teach him to be independent, nurture his character and help him develop resilience. He will also probably take after you in the way you speak, how you interact with your partner, how you treat others and how you cope with stress as well as adversities.

**Lessons Learnt**

Life is full of surprises and miracles. Children are a miracle, make time for your little ones.

## Chapter 44

### Compatibility is key
*"For me, compatibility is a sense of humor, being able to laugh together; that is very important."* – Felicity Kendal

**Coffee with Sophia**

*"Some say compatibility is overrated. I say, the lack of, can break relationships. A similar sense of humor, compatibility in the way you fight, in bed...views on having kids, location to live, values. Take these away and you will end up being conflicted. How much are you willing to give up for love? Are you okay with giving up on having babies or having sex once a week when you need more? Can you live with an avoidant partner when you actually need someone who can deal with difficult conversations maturely? Do you want someone who will quit their job and live off you while you give your all to building a career and financial security for your family?"*

**Thought of the day**

All is good when you get married until you realize that he doesn't come to bed by twelve and stays up till four in the morning. You don't get to have breakfasts together on weekends. You are sleep deprived because the noise from his computer games and tv wakes you up at night. You treat yourself to a nice meal when you achieve little wins.

However, your financially conservative partner is reluctant to spend, causing your celebrations to be punctuated with vibes of disapproval.

Now that you are ready to have children, he is hesitant. He wants to relocate to a suburb but you are just on your way up the corporate ladder in the city. You believe in making plans to manage your life better but he prefers to improvise. You go to church on Sundays and you see other couples spending time together in the house of God, but he doesn't believe that God exists.

You love him but you are not quite happy with how things are going and you are not sure if this is going to work in the long run.

How compatible are you with your partner, what are your common grounds and are there any deal breakers?

1. Sense of humor
2. Wanting children
3. Location you want to live in
4. Values
5. Sexuality
6. Bedtime habits
7. Fighting
8. How you spend your money
9. Drinking habits
10. Smoking
11. Supporting your parents

**Lessons Learnt**

Compatibility is important in a relationship. Common grounds can lessen the strain as you complement each other without having to compromise all the time.

# Chapter 45

## Maintain healthy boundaries
*"A lack of boundaries invites a lack of respect." –*
*Anonymous*

## Coffee with Sophia

*"You have every right to assert your personal boundaries because if you don't, others will step all over you. When you make allowance for people to take a piss on you and you let that slide, what sort of message are you sending them? That it is OK for them to take a piss on you. They will do it over and over again. You need to have a good sense of self and respect; put people in their places if they cross the line."*

## Thought of the day

A relationship is like a tango between to people, they test their boundaries with each other every now and then.

I believe that when you love someone, all you want is for them to be happy. But once in a while, you will push the envelope to get him to give in to you. You persuade him, you negotiate and whoops, you sometimes cross the line. Admittedly, we all make that mistake.

A couple of areas you can be mindful of when it comes to keeping healthy boundaries:

1. Privacy – mobile, email, letters, social media
2. Career, workplace, colleagues, bosses
3. Parents, siblings
4. Exes, children from other marriages
5. Sexual boundaries
6. Time set out for friends, self
7. Fighting with boundaries – avoid name-calling, character assassinating, emasculating him
8. Staying faithful
9. Restriction of his personal freedom – expression, fashion, spending, mobility, choices

Even if it feels like pulling teeth getting anything out of your partner or getting your way, it is important to be mindful that you respect his personal boundaries. If he says no, respect that. Similarly, maintain your boundaries and don't become a doormat yourself either.

**Lessons Learnt**

There are some lines that cannot be crossed in relationships. Maintain a healthy set of boundaries in your relationship, respect his and assert yours.

# Chapter 46

## Do not lose yourself, keep your own identity in your relationship

*"A wise man never loses anything if he has himself." –
Michel de Montaigne*

### Coffee with Sophia

*"A woman in love is like a woman on a sinking ship. She starts throwing things out of the ship – pride, dignity, self-respect, self-love, her identity. You fall so deeply in love that you try so hard to become the woman he wants you to be. One day, when you look into the mirror, you won't recognize the person looking back at you anymore."*

### Thought of the day

It is easy to fall deeply in love and lose ourselves if we forget to keep our own identity in the pursuit of love. Though it can be important to keep your partner happy and meet him halfway, it shouldn't mean that you should lose your individuality.

1. Take time for yourself
2. Take time to do things that you like
3. Maintain your circle of friends
4. Stay connected with your family to stay rooted
5. Maintain a set of healthy boundaries in your relationship

6. Maintain a healthy sense of self-respect and self-love
7. Stay dignified
8. Exercise self-control
9. Help your partner understand your preferences and needs

Having that sense of self is important for a woman. Even when you are deeply in love with another, you want to safeguard your dignity, self-love and self-esteem.

**Lessons Learnt**

Follow your heart but don't lose yourself in the process.

# Chapter 47

## Build a friendship with your lover

*"It is not the lack of love, but a lack of friendship that makes unhappy marriages." – Friedrich Nietzsche*

### Coffee with Sophia

*"Have you read about how some relationships can fare better when the couple meet as housemates, classmates or colleagues? They meet the person first and have no expectation as opposed to starting out as lovers. Of course, they have some chemistry to begin with. My wife and I are first best friends, then lovers. I can tell her everything as she makes it safe for me to share anything with her, she doesn't judge...she listens."*

### Thought of the day

We get together with someone and we start to have expectations of how he needs to behave as a partner, a lover. We forget that he is a person, just like your best friend who talks to you on the phone every week.

Building a friendship with your lover is important, it allows you to be more comfortable in your own skin. You work better together in a team and you will be less quick to judge. Conversations can be fun, light and less focused on what is right or wrong with the relationship, the in-laws and the kids.

However, it doesn't mean that you turn your lover into a roommate. I have met many couples who shared that they feel like they are living with a roommate and friend - the passion was completely gone.

Finding that balance - the right level of friendship with your lover and keeping the passion alive in your relationship - will be key.

**Lessons Learnt**

Build a friendship with your lover.

# Chapter 48

## Be responsible for your own happiness

*"Giving someone else the responsibility of guarding your own happiness, is like letting a lion babysit your toddler."* – *Sophia Brooke*

### Coffee with Sophia

*"When I was single, I thought that finding someone will make me happier. I gave up control of my happiness and delegated it to my partner. It became a pendulum. My life can be going great but it can also turn the minute my partner has a bad day."*

### Thought of the day

Happiness comes from within.

Too many of us allow our happiness to be affected by other people, events and things. We let anxiety, sadness and anger engulf us.

A philosopher, *Michel de Montaigne* said of anxiety and anger, *"Wretched is the mind anxious about the future." "There is no point getting angry at events, they are indifferent to our wraths."*

Being happy is an art, you need to take charge of how you feel as happiness comes from within.

1. Practice gratitude – write down three things that you are grateful for every day. Practicing gratitude is said to be able to increase your level of happiness.
2. Smile – if you feel sad, smile. Smiling is said to activate some chemicals in the brain that makes us happy. It can be counter-intuitive, but try forcing a smile when you feel sad, and you will probably feel better right after.
3. Stay positive and expect the best outcome
4. Remove negativity in your life
5. Surround yourself with good people and minimize contact with unsafe people
6. Love yourself
7. Embrace changes
8. Have the courage to change when you think it best for you to do so
9. Don't take yourself too seriously
10. Let go of the past
11. Learn to forgive yourself and others
12. Live life mindfully
13. Take charge of your own happiness
14. Accept yourself

**Lessons Learnt**

It is only when you are happy, that you can make others around you happy. Take charge of your own happiness.

## Chapter 49

### Marriage – for better or for worse

*"Marriage is not just spiritual communion and passionate embraces; marriage is also three meals a day and remembering to carry out the trash." – Dr. Joyce Brothers*

**Coffee with Sophia**

A reporter once asked a couple, *"How did you manage to stay together for 65 years?"* The woman replied, *"We were born in a time when if something was broken, we would fix it, not throw it away..."*

**Thought of the day**

Just two generations ago, our grandparents used to fix things that were broken. They mended clothes, shoes, pots and pans. Resources were scarce and people were more appreciative.

Today, we buy disposable paper plates, utensils and paper napkins. We throw them away after one use. There's so much options when it comes to food, things or even people. When people have more options, they tend to believe that they can get away with bad behaviors and that they can replace their partners easily.

Marriage is a commitment, a holy communion of two people who promised to stay together, no matter what. In times of crisis, stress may get the better of you or your partner. But, don't lose faith. It is especially important during these times that you remember your vows to each other.

1. Understand that most couples will experience at least one severe life crisis.
2. Know that stresses can sometimes get the better of your partner.
3. Sort out financial problems together.
4. Understand that unemployment can be short-lived if you both have the right attitude. Encourage each other through your job searches.
5. Understand that relocation, moving, having children or a partner falling ill, can be stressful. Do not let that affect your marriage.
6. Understand that your in-laws may be a pain in the ass, but maintain your boundaries and do not let them pull you apart.
7. Avoid putting yourself in a position that will cause you to be unfaithful.
8. Have faith and trust in your partner.
9. Renew your love and marriage vows.
10. Embrace the aging process as you grow old together.

There is nothing more beautiful than seeing two people face the world together and thrive amidst adversity in a team.

## Lessons Learnt

*"...to have and to hold, from this day forward, for better, for worse, for richer, for poorer, in sickness and in health, to love and to cherish, till death do us part...and this is my solemn vow."*

# Chapter 50

## And one more thing – unremitting kindness
*"Be kind, for everyone you meet is fighting a hard battle." -
Plato*

### Coffee with Sophia

*"I think, people should retain the perspective that we are all
frail creatures who deserve a break once in a while,
because sooner or later, we all fuck up. I believe that the
core thing that makes a relationship work full time is
unremitting kindness, on both sides. Obviously, you both
have to be able to laugh your heads off often, dance naked
in the rain and retain awe at all the wonderful things in
life."*

### Thought of the day

It is not uncommon for couples that have been together for a
long time to be kinder to a stranger than to each other.

You get comfortable with your partner, you set lofty
standards and you impose unreasonable expectations. You
look for hairline cracks in his character, his actions and his
words. You want him to be strong for you, to be a better
husband and to be a better father.

But, what about kindness? Are you kind to him when he
fails to meet your expectation? Do you know that

sometimes, even when his smile, he may be battling with something that he doesn't share with anyone including you?

1. Choose kindness when he falters
2. If he falls, lift him up instead of pushing him down further
3. When he is in pain, comfort him
4. When he fails to live up to your expectation, manage your expectation, give him time
5. If he feels inadequate in one way or the other, be supportive and avoid rubbing it in
6. Don't make things worse for him than it is
7. Don't make life unnecessarily difficult for the both of you

Love is kindness. When you love someone, you can be kind to him simply by being there for him, by showing your sympathy. You remember the person you love even when he is at his lowest point and is not able to be himself. When you sometimes think that he least deserves your kindness, those are probably the times when he needs it most.

**Lessons Learnt**

Sooner or later, we all mess up. And when we do, remember this one more thing - unremitting kindness.

Printed in Great Britain
by Amazon